GOLD

by Gail Beck

Table of Contents

Pictures To Think About

Words To Think About

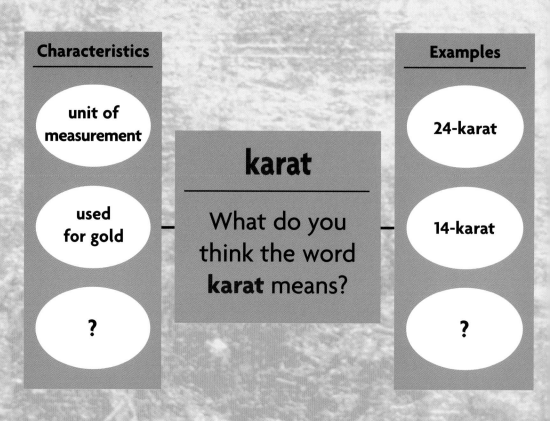

Characteristics

- unit of measurement
- used for gold
- ?

karat

What do you think the word **karat** means?

Examples

- 24-karat
- 14-karat
- ?

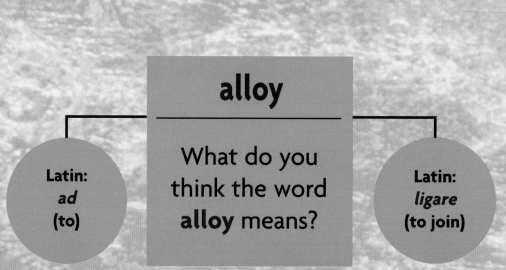

alloy

What do you think the word **alloy** means?

Latin: *ad* (to)

Latin: *ligare* (to join)

corrode

What do you think the word **corrode** means?

What can cause something to **corrode**?

What are some things that **corrode**?

air	?	acid

iron	?	wood

iv

Introduction

You win a contest. The prize is a gold medal. You feel the weight of the solid gold in your hand. You are proud of your new medal. Why is gold special?

Gold is a symbol of excellence, or greatness. It is also a symbol of wealth. People use gold as money. People also use gold to make jewelry. Gold is a precious (PREH-shus) metal. It is very valuable.

▼ Kelly Holmes wo
two Olympic gol
medals in 2004.

The word *gold* comes from an Old English word. The word *geolo* means "yellow." This yellow metal is not just found in money or jewelry. Gold has other uses. Gold is in machines. Gold is in cell phones and computers. It is also in some medicines.

In this book, you will learn about gold. You will learn how people find gold. You will see how people mine, or dig, for it. You will also see why gold is valuable. Read on. Discover precious gold.

✔ POINT

MAKE CONNECTIONS

Write the word **gold** on a sheet of paper. Then make a list of objects you've seen or heard of that are made of gold. Put a check mark beside any you read about in this book.

3

What Is Gold?

Gold is a **mineral** (MIH-nuh-rul). Minerals are solid materials found in rocks. Earth has many minerals. Silver and iron are minerals. What makes gold different?

Gold has certain **properties** (PRAH-per-teez). A property is something that can be measured or seen. Color and weight are properties. How much something can bend is a property. Being shiny or dull is a property.

Gold has been used ▲ to make jewelry for thousands of years. This gold pendant is from Colombia.

Physical Properties

Gold's yellow color is a physical (FIH-zih-kul) property. You can see the color. The symbol for gold is Au. The symbol comes from the Latin word *aurum*. This word means "shining dawn." People compare gold's yellow color to the sun.

Gold has a bright **luster** (LUS-ter), or shine. Gold is also **malleable** (MA-lee-uh-bul). It is a soft metal. Gold is easy to hammer or press into different shapes. People use gold to make jewelry.

MATH MATTERS

Gold is measured in troy ounces. One troy ounce is equivalent to 1.1 ounces (31.1 grams). This chart shows the average price of 1 troy ounce of gold between 1805 and 2005.

Rising Gold Prices

Dollars (y-axis): 0, 100, 200, 300, 400, 500, 600
Year (x-axis): 1805, 1855, 1905, 1955, 2005

▲ gold

Chemical Properties

Gold also has chemical (KEH-mih-kul) properties. Gold is an **element** (EH-leh-ment). An element is a pure substance. You cannot break it down into anything smaller. Gold is stable. It does not mix easily with other elements.

Gold does not **corrode** (kuh-RODE), or wear away. Gold does not rust like iron. Gold is not changed by water or oxygen. Gold can last for years at the bottom of the sea. Gold also keeps its shine.

▲ Gold does not corrode the way other metals do.

Gold Alloys

Gold is a soft metal. People mix gold with other metals to make gold stronger. A metal mixture is called an **alloy** (A-loy). Gold can be mixed with silver and copper. A whiter, stronger alloy results.

Gold can also be in a **compound** (KAHM-pownd). A compound is a substance made of two or more elements.

EVERYDAY SCIENCE

Common Compounds

The salt in your kitchen is a compound. The water in your sink is a compound. This table shows what makes up each compound. The chemical formula uses chemical symbols to describe the compound.

Substance	Composition of each compound	Chemical formula
Table salt	1 sodium atom + 1 chlorine atom	NaCl
Water	2 hydrogen atoms + 1 oxygen atom	H_2O

Where Do You Find Gold?

You can find tiny bits of gold everywhere. Gold is in almost all rocks and soil. Even seawater has some gold in it. But that gold is not easy to extract, or take out.

Most gold is found in Earth's **crust** (KRUST). The crust is Earth's rocky outer layer. The crust is the ground you walk on. It is the mountains, the river bottoms, and the ocean floor.

The layer below Earth's crust is called the **mantle** (MAN-tul). The mantle is very hot. The mantle is made of **magma** (MAG-muh), or melted rock. Magma has different elements. One of these elements is gold.

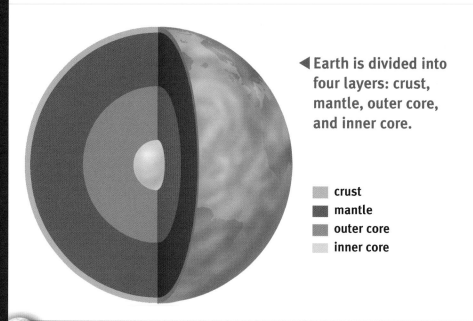

◀ Earth is divided into four layers: crust, mantle, outer core, and inner core.

crust
mantle
outer core
inner core

How does gold get in the crust? Scientists have a few theories, or ideas. Magma is always pushing up against the crust. Some scientists think that magma pushes into cracks in the crust. The liquid magma has gold in it.

As magma enters the crust, the magma cools. The magma begins to harden into solid rock. Gold does not mix easily with other elements. Instead, gold mixes with other pieces of gold. The gold cools into solid chunks.

HISTORICAL PERSPECTIVE

Seawater contains gold. The gold is dissolved in the water. Scientists estimate that there are approximately 0.1 to 2 milligrams of gold dissolved in each metric ton of seawater. In the 1950s, the Dow Chemical Company tried to isolate gold from fifteen tons of seawater. The company spent $50,000 on the project, but they were able to extract only 0.09 milligram of gold. They realized that getting gold from seawater was not worth the cost.

The shiny yellow ▶ specks inside this rock are gold.

Some scientists have another theory. They think that rain helps bring gold up into the crust. Rain drips through cracks in Earth's crust. As the water travels downward, it hits hot spots. The water begins to boil. The boiling water dissolves gold and other metals in the rock.

In time, the water and dissolved gold push upward through cracks in the crust. As it cools, gold separates from the water. The gold cools in rocky cracks. Thin lines of gold form.

▼ Miners search for these veins of gold.

A rock that contains gold is called **ore** (OR). Gold ore can be found in different places. It is very rare, though. Sometimes miners have to dig up tons of rock to find just 1 ounce (28 grams) of gold. Mining gold is hard work.

Eyewitness Account

Around 1880, Taam Sze Pui, a Chinese miner, went to Australia when gold was discovered there. Here's what he said about looking for gold: *"To search for gold is to look for the moon at the bottom of the sea."*

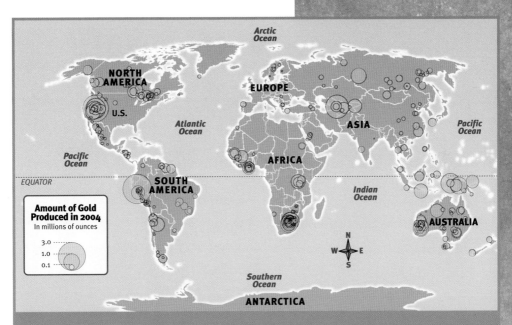

▲ People mine for gold all over the world.

Mining for Gold

▲ This geologist is surveying an area and studying the rocks to find gold.

Today, people still search for gold. People find and mine gold in different ways.

First, geologists (jee-AH-luh-jists) survey an area of land. These scientists study the land. The scientists take samples of the rocks and minerals. Then they find out what the rocks are made of. They use their findings to map out where the gold is. Once they know, mining can start.

Miners dig underground tunnels. They also dig large, open pits. Then they blast the rock into pieces. The miners haul, or carry, the rock pieces to the surface. Then they sort the pieces.

Miners pick out rocks that have bits of gold. Then they must extract the gold from the rocks. Companies have different ways to remove gold from rock.

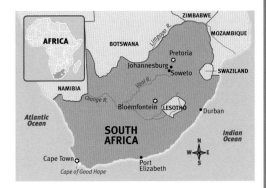

▲ Since the 1880s, South Africa has been the largest supplier of the world's gold. However, it is producing less and less gold each year.

▼ Miners dig for gold in open pit mines.

Extracting Gold

One way to extract gold is to use chemicals. Cyanide (SY-uh-nide) is a poisonous chemical.

Gold does not react with most chemicals. But gold dissolves when it touches cyanide. Miners treat rocks with a cyanide solution, or liquid. The gold dissolves into the solution. Then it drains out of the rocks. The gold is taken out of the solution. Then miners refine the extracted gold. It becomes cleaned, pure gold.

The problem with this method is cyanide. This chemical is not safe. It harms the environment.

They Made a DIFFERENCE

When cyanide seeps into waterways, it can harm marine life and human health. In 2004, a corporation planned to open a gold mine near Cajamarca, Peru. When local residents heard about the plan, they became fearful. Father Marco Arana, a local priest, led a nonviolent campaign against the mine. His efforts worked. The mine was not built near Cajamarca. Arana won his nation's highest human-rights award.

▲ Father Marco Arana

HOW GOLD IS REMOVED FROM ORE

gold ore is crushed
to a powder

gold mixes with
cyanide to form pulp

pulp

coarse gold
returned to mill

crusher

mill

screen separates
gold from pulp

cyclone separates
out coarse gold

hot cyanide
solution

gold-bearing
carbon

gold is dissolved in
cyanide solution

carbon is
stripped out

screen

stripped
carbon

carbon grains collect gold

recycled
solution

chemical called flux
melts steel wool

steel wool melted

gold-coated
steel wool

flux

gold is separated from
solution using steel wool

molten or soft gold
poured into molds

gold bars

casting

15

The History of Gold

People have valued gold for a long time. Scientists think that gold was the first metal humans used. People made gold into jewelry and decorations.

Where did people find gold long ago? Early people often found placer gold. This is gold that has been washed away from lode gold. Lode gold is gold found in rocks.

▲ The earliest known gold jewelry belonged to the Sumerian Queen Pu-abi. She lived in the area that is now the Middle East.

IT'S A FACT

One Egyptian king claimed the gold in ancient Egypt was as "common as dust." Egypt was a major gold-producing area for much of its history.

Tutankhamen ▶

▲ The ancient Greeks used gold for jewelry.

How does placer gold wash away? Water in rivers and streams moves quickly. As moving water passes over rocks, the rocks erode. As the rocks wear away, any gold bits wash downstream. Some of the gold gets stuck in sandy riverbeds. Sometimes the gold shines in the sunlight.

Long ago, people began to find gold in sandy rivers. They picked up the sand. They washed the sand through sheepskin. Any gold stuck to the woolly fleece. Then the fleece was dried and burned. When the fire burned out, tiny globs of melted gold were left behind.

EVERYDAY SCIENCE

Panning is an old method that is still used for finding placer gold. The miner scoops the river deposits into the pan. Then the miner puts the pan partially under water and moves it in a circular motion. The lighter river particles wash away. The heavier gold particles fall to the bottom of the pan.

During the 1500s, many European countries sent ships out to explore distant lands. People sought new places to conquer. People also searched for gold. They used gold as money.

Hernando de Cortéz (air-NAHN-doh DAY kor-TEZ) was a Spanish explorer. In 1519, Cortéz sailed to Mexico. The Aztec empire was there. This empire was rich with gold. Cortéz and his men conquered the Aztec. Then they took the gold. Cortéz melted down the gold into gold bars. The gold made Spain a very rich country.

▲ This map from 1524 shows the Aztec's main city, Tenochtitlán. The Aztec empire was rich with gold.

▲ This is an alchemy lab. Alchemists considered gold the purest substance on Earth.

Alchemy

Long ago, people looked for ways to change other metals into gold. This study was called alchemy (AL-keh-mee). Alchemists thought they could change lead into gold.

In the 1700s, scientists learned more about elements and their properties. They found out that they could not change other metals into gold. In time, alchemy died out.

IT'S A FACT

The mineral pyrite is bright yellow. Many people mistake it for gold. It's known as "fool's gold."

How Gold Is Used

Gold is beautiful and valuable. Did you know that it is also very useful? You can find gold inside a cell phone or computer. What is gold doing there? Keep reading to find out.

Most metals are **ductile** (DUK-til). That means you can make them into wire. Gold is the most ductile metal on Earth. You can turn 1 troy ounce of gold into 50 miles (80 kilometers) of wire!

▼ There is gold in your video game system.

All metals conduct, or carry, electricity. After copper and silver, gold is the best metal at conducting electricity.

Your computer or cell phone has many tiny electronic parts. Each part does a different job. For your machine to work, the parts need to connect. Gold wires often do that job.

▲ Computers use gold wiring.

CAREERS IN SCIENCE

Computer engineers design computers. They also create machines that need a computer to operate, such as a robot. Some computer engineers write software programs that tell a computer what to do. A computer game is an example of software. Engineers who design computers usually major in computer or electrical engineering in college. Software engineers have degrees in computer science or software engineering.

Gold in Dentistry

Gold has other uses. It can give you a truly bright smile. Long ago, people began to use gold in their teeth. Some people also used gold wire to hold false teeth in place.

In 1530, the first book on dentistry appeared in Germany. It said to use gold to fill cavities. Why is gold good for filling cavities or making false teeth?

▲ Today, dentists continue to put gold in their patients' teeth.

Gold does not corrode, or break down. Gold does not react with oxygen. Gold is also safe to use inside the human body.

Because of the high price of gold, dentists today do not use gold often. Most dentists use less costly metals for filling cavities.

IT'S A FACT

Ever since the 1920s, doctors have been using gold to help treat patients with rheumatoid arthritis. This disease causes a person to develop swelling and stiffness of the joints. Some patients take a form of gold by injection or pill to help relieve joint pain and swelling.

Gold in Space

Gold has another great use. Gold helps keep astronauts safe in outer space.

Space is a dangerous place. The sun is very powerful. The sun sends out high levels of radiation (ray-dee-AY-shun).

Earth has an atmosphere (AT-muh-sfeer). This thick layer of gas surrounds Earth. It blocks some of the sun's harmful rays. In space, there is no atmosphere.

There is gold in this ▶ spacesuit.

The sun's rays can cause a person's body to overheat. Radiation can cause cancer. Astronauts wear space suits. The suits protect them from the sun.

The visors on space helmets are coated with gold. The gold reflects the sun's rays. This keeps an astronaut's head cool and safe.

Gold also protects spacecraft. The first landers that people used to land on the moon were coated with gold. The gold shielded the equipment from radiation.

▲ This is the lunar lander used by the first astronauts to set foot on the moon. It had gold-coated sides.

PRIMARY SOURCE

"On July 20, 1969, astronauts Neil Armstrong and Buzz Aldrin became the first humans to land on the moon. They were protected by gold-coated visors."
— *The New York Times,* July 21, 1969

Gold as Decoration

Gold is the most malleable metal. That means it bends easily. That is why people make gold into jewelry and other items.

Take 1 troy ounce of gold. You can hammer it into a 300-square-foot (28-square-meter) sheet. This sheet is called gold leaf. Gold leaf can be as thin as 0.000005 inch (0.000127 millimeter). That is 400 times thinner than a strand of hair. Gold leaf can be shaped into many beautiful things.

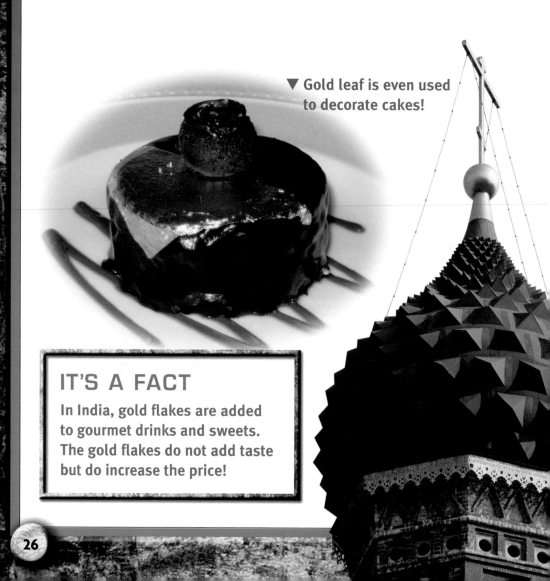

▼ Gold leaf is even used to decorate cakes!

IT'S A FACT

In India, gold flakes are added to gourmet drinks and sweets. The gold flakes do not add taste but do increase the price!

As you know, gold is often mixed with other metals. The combination makes gold stronger. It also changes gold's color. How can you tell how much gold is actually in a piece of jewelry?

A **karat** (KAIR-ut) is a unit of measurement. A karat measures how pure gold is. A piece of jewelry marked 24 karat, or 24kt, is pure gold. A piece marked 1 karat is only one part gold. The remaining twenty-three parts of the alloy are other metals.

✔ POINT REREAD

The introduction says gold is special, a symbol of excellence and wealth. Page 20 says gold is beautiful and useful. What other words and phrases can you find that describe gold? Which one best sums up what you've learned? Why?

MATH MATTERS

This chart shows the percent of gold for each karat level. Which of the following do you think costs more: an ounce of 18kt gold or an ounce of 14kt gold?

Karat	Percent Gold
24kt	100%
18kt	75%
14kt	58.3%
10kt	41.6%

▲ The World Cup Trophy is made of 18-karat gold. What percent of the trophy is not gold?

Conclusion

Gold is a mineral. Gold is a natural substance found in Earth's crust. It has certain properties. It has a yellow color. It is also shiny and malleable. Gold is prized for its beauty. Long ago, ancient people began turning the bright yellow metal into decorative things.

▲ People have worn gold jewelry for thousands of years.

Today, people use gold for more than just jewelry. Dentists use gold to fill cavities. Astronauts use gold to protect themselves from the sun. Gold conducts electricity. That makes it valuable for use in technology. People also use gold as money.

Throughout history, people have searched for gold. Today, people still mine for gold. Mining for gold can hurt the environment. People are looking for new ways to mine gold. These new ways need to be safe. They also need to work well.

Gold Throughout History

Time Line

This time line highlights the role of gold throughout history.

3000 B.C.	The Sumer civilization creates decorative gold items.
1200 B.C.	People use sheepskin to trap gold particles.
600s B.C.	People use gold wire to hold false teeth in place.
1511	Spanish rulers send explorers to search for gold.
1521	Spanish explorer Hernando de Cortéz destroys the Aztec empire in Mexico and claims their gold.
1530	The first book on dentistry, printed in Germany, recommends using gold to fill cavities.
1887	Scientists discover how to use cyanide to extract gold from its ore.
1927	Scientists use gold to help treat patients with rheumatoid arthritis.
1950s	Dow Chemical Company spends $50,000 to extract 0.09 milligram of gold from 15 tons of seawater.
1968	A tiny computer chip is created that contains 1,024 points that are connected by gold.
1969	Astronauts land on the moon wearing gold-coated visors to protect them from solar radiation. The moon lander is covered with protective gold sheets.
2001	Companies around the world use about 200 tons of gold to make electronic parts.
2004	Father Marco Arana leads a nonviolent campaign against mining plans in Cajamarca, Peru. Local residents fear that the mine may harm human and environmental health.

Glossary

alloy   (A-loy) a mixture of two or more metals (page 7)

compound   (KAHM-pownd) a substance formed by the chemical combination of two or more elements (page 7)

corrode   (kuh-RODE) to wear away, little by little (page 6)

crust   (KRUST) Earth's outermost layer (page 8)

ductile   (DUK-til) easily formed into wire (page 20)

element   (EH-leh-ment) a pure substance that can't be broken down into simpler substances (page 6)

karat   (KAIR-ut) a unit of measure for the fineness of gold (page 27)

luster   (LUS-ter) a bright shine (page 5)

magma   (MAG-muh) liquid rock under Earth's crust (page 8)

malleable   (MA-lee-uh-bul) able to be made into different shapes by hammering or rolling (page 5)

mantle   (MAN-tul) Earth's layer between the crust and the outer core (page 8)

mineral   (MIH-nuh-rul) a solid substance found in nature that has a crystal structure (page 4)

ore   (OR) a rock that contains a valuable metal (page 11)

property   (PRAH-per-tee) a characteristic of matter that can be observed or measured (page 4)

Index